Riddles for Kids

Brain Teasers and Trick Questions for Kids & Families

Author: Martha Astin

Table of Contents

Introduction

Riddles are a wholesome, fun, and learning-filled activity both for kids and adults alike. They are a perfect and entertaining way to pass the time during parties, family get-togethers, and picnics. Even if you are planning to go on trips with college friends, playing riddles is a great way to pass time and also improve lateral and logical thinking capabilities.

Having a riddle book handy when it is your turn to babysit at home while your spouse has the night out is the best way to keep the kids engaged and quiet even as you break your head trying to answer some hard-level riddles. In these days of overwhelming dependence on electronic gadgets and video games, sitting with a book and solving puzzles is a scintillating idea instead of playing mindless games on the screen that can not only hurt your eyes but can also dull your thinking capabilities.

Your brain works like a muscle. The more you exercise it, the sharper and stronger it will get. So, get yourself ready to crack some easy, some not-so-easy, and a few hard riddles.

Level 1: Riddles #1-100

Question #1

A skeleton that makes you laugh is called _____

Question #2

What has 4 legs and a body and yet cannot walk?

Question #3

I bounce, flip, and throw myself around on the floor (sometimes on bars or sticks too) so much that it looks like I have no bones. I need a white powder for perfection. Who am I?

Question #4

I have space but no rooms, keys but no doors. I let you enter, but you can never leave. What am I?

Question #5

The home of a ghost family has all rooms except one. Which one?

Question #6

Can you make SIX into an odd number without doing any arithmetic operations?

Question #7

I carry a lot of news and secrets. I walk, drive, or cycle to work every day (come rain or shine) to deliver what I pick up to a place that is fixed beforehand. I usually wear a uniform. Who am I?

Question #8

What is the favorite swimming place for ghosts and zombies?

Question #9

What water can you chew and eat?

Question #10

I get paid to laugh, cry, be a hero who flies around in the sky, be a demon, a saint, or anything else. Who am I?

Question #11

After some booming and zapping, I emerge beautiful and radiant.Everyone is mesmerized by me. Some people say I

9

have lots of wealth hidden. But no one has seen it. What am I?

Question #12

Dracula loves this so much that he saves it in a bank. What is it?

Question #13

I come in solid and liquid forms and most of the time, I create bubbles. There is no home, which does not have me. What am I?

Question #14

I give you problems only so that you can get better at what you do. I also help you solve the same problems that I gave you. I may be good at math or science or both. I could also sing and dance well. Even though I am a bit strict, I love you very much. Who am I?

Question #15

This thing is hard, cold, and surrounds even a cemetery. What is it?

Question #16

Why did Adam and Eve not have a date?

Question #17

I am a mother with no sons, daughters, or even a husband. Who am I?

Question #18

I am used in nearly every sport and come in different colors and sizes and patterns. I share a name with a state in the US. What am I?

Question #19

If you were to cross a Dracula and a teacher, what will you get?

Question #20

I can display many emotions, expressions, and faces. I am just a click or tap away. What am I?

Question #21

I have legs, arms, and a body but no guts. What am I?

Question #22

You can use this word to express a fruit, a bird, and a person. Which word?

Question #23

I have many branches but no leaves or fruits or roots. I may not be green but I hold green things in my belly. What am I?

Question #24

I can fly myself and people around the world, but am not a bird. I am surrounded by metals and I have a very responsible job. Who am I?

Question #25

Where do ghosts, mummies, and zombies go to take a break from their work?

Question #26

I am a bee that doesn't sting and you can pass me around. What bee am I?

Question #27

I go up and down. Sometimes I'm curvy, or sometimes I'm straight. Sometimes I'm simple, and sometimes I'm grand. Without me you can never go up or down. What am I?

Question #28

I can be a major or a minor. But it is important to get the right key before you touch me. What am I?

Question #29

I cycle round and round without stopping and never get tired. What am I?

Question #30

Famous people never sweat. Do you know why?

Question #31

A girl goes to the local grocery store and buys a dozen eggs. On her way back home, she falls down and hurts herself. Also, all except three of the eggs break. How many are remaining?

Question #32

In a one-floor home, the living room was purple, the bedrooms were yellow and green, the bathrooms were white, and the outside color was grey. What color was the staircase?

Question #33

Friday, John and James have lunch together. The bill was $24, which is equally shared by the friends. John and James have $8 each. Who paid the third part?

Question #34

Use only the number 6 and the addition operation to get the answer 750.

Question #35

The following people go to have coffee: one grandfather, two fathers, and two sons. They each had one cup of coffee and yet ordered for only 3 cups. How is this possible?

Question #36

If I shift my position even by a few inches, I can create widespread destruction killing people and damaging property. I am really big and yet remain invisible. What am I?

Question #37

Find an 8-letter word that works like this- take away one letter at a time, and you will be left with a new word each time until you reach the final one word. Remember all the words make sense!

Question #38

I can fill a home or your mouth or any space available to me. But you can never catch me in your hands. What am I?

Question #39

I sleep during the day, and I am awake at night. I can fly but have no feathers. Many people are scared of me. What am I?

Question #40

The more you take of this item, the more you leave behind. What is this item?

Question #41

What has ears but cannot hear a single sound?

Question #42

Name three consecutive days without using the names of the days of the week.

Question #43

What types of tables do not have legs?

Question #44

What drink is typically added to your cereal?

Question #45

This food can be grown without sun or soil. However, some of them can be nutritious while others can be poisonous. What is this food item?

Question #46

If you strip out my skin, you will find my flesh, which is sweet or sour. Some throw away my peel while others use it in their dishes. What am I?

Question #47

What is a home that has 5 apples and 10 blackberries called?

Question #48

What kind of precious stones do you find in a deck of cards?

Question #49

This thing has a tail, a head, but no body. It is brown in color. What is it?

Question #50

I travel all over the world and visit nearly every country on this earth. Yet, I can never leave my corner. What am I?

Question #51

Find a word that looks the same upside down or straight or sideways.

Question #52

There is something that comes once every minute, twice in a moment, but never in a hundred years. What is this?

Question #53

There is a word that is spelled incorrectly. Which is that word?

Question #54

How can you drop an egg but ensure you don't break it?

Question #55

A handy word for measuring and also for running a kingdom. What is this word?

Question #56

It was Christmas morning in New York and when a mother came back from grocery shopping, she saw that someone has eaten all the food she'd cooked. Her three sons and husband said they were each busy with some work and did not eat the food.

The eldest son said he was mowing the lawn. The second son said he was watching TV. The third son said he was exercising. The father said he was reading the newspaper. Who was lying and had actually eaten the food?

Question #57

What can be white, dirty, small, big, and wicked?

Question #58

What is never present now and is always late?

Question #59

What is that thing which even if you stamped on it will never get dirty? In fact, if you tried to wash it, you couldn't.

Question #60

What would the name of the classic film Tron if it were remade now?

Question #61

This chemical element never follows. Which one?

Question #62

Which weighs more? A pound of feathers or a pound of cotton?

Question #63

I sit alongside the gas neon and am a gas just like my family member neon. I am also the name of a super hero's home. What am I?

Question #64

Two chemical elements when combined heal? Which two?

Question #65

Which is the largest of the following: circle, triangle, square, rectangle.

Question #66

How can you get the smell of roses, apple, blueberries, and pumpkin without actually lighting them on fire?

Question #67

I can be dark or white. I am sometimes bitter and sometimes sweet. I come in cookies and cakes, what am I?

Question #68

You can cut me, dice me, chop me, or slice me. Still, you are one to cry. What am I?

Question #69

I can be small or big and am usually on the ceiling or wall. I do what the sun does but in a much smaller way. What am I?

Question #70

Why is it not possible for your nose to be 12 inches in length?

Question #71

What is yellow and has the smell of green paint?

Question #72

What are ducks' favorite food?

Question #73

What is the name of the tree that we carry in our hands?

Question #74

This thing has many eyes and yet cannot see. What is it?

Question #75

You can hold this thing in your right hand but never in your left hand? What is it?

Question #76

This kind of fish chases mice. Which kind?

Question #77

I shave multiple times each day and yet my beard remains the same. Who am I?

Question #78

An engineer and a girl go camping outdoors. The girl was the engineer's daughter, but the engineer was not the girl's mother. How is this possible?

Question #79

What did the bed sheet say to the scared cot?

Question #80

I'm holding a bee in my hand. What is in my eyes?

Question #81

Only this kind of coat can you put on when it's wet. Which kind?

Question #82

A man goes to his bathroom, looks at the mirror, and shoots himself in the mouth. Yet, he walks out unharmed. How is this possible?

Question #83

What never lets you go but is always pulling you down?

Question #84

A rooster climbs all the way up a hill from the northern side and lays an egg on top. Which way will the egg roll down?

Question #85

A lady kills her husband and hides the body near the edge of the forest. A few days later the cops find the body and call the lady saying that her husband is dead and to come quickly to the scene of the crime. She hangs up the phone and rushes to the place and the cops arrest her. How do they know she was the murderer?

Question #86

Imagine you are falling from an airplane without a parachute. How can you stop yourself from getting hurt or dying?

Question #87

This item works in a unique way. When you need it you throw it over and put it away when you don't need it. What is it?

Question #88

A man jumped from a helicopter without a parachute and still didn't get seriously hurt. How is this possible?

Question #89

Three men are rowing a boat when suddenly it capsizes. All fall into the water and swim to safety. However, only two of the three people's hair gets wet. How is this possible?

Question #90

The person who makes this item does not need it. The person who buys it will not use it. The person who uses it will not see or feel it. What is it?

Question #91

When I am young, I stand tall and when I grow old and weak, I become short. What am I?

Question #92

What has two hands but can never clap?

Question #93

What has an eye but is still blind and cannot see?

Question #94

You drop me from the tallest building in town and nothing will happen to me. But, if you were to drop me in water, I will die. What am I?

Question #95

The more it dries the wetter it gets. What is it?

Question #96

This animal walks on fours in the morning, on two in the afternoon, and on three in the evening? Which animal are we talking about?

Question #97

Betty, the butcher, is 5 feet tall and her shop assistant is over 6 feet and wears size 12 shoes. What do the shop assistant and Betty weigh?

Question #98

It is difficult not to share me with others, but once you share me I don't belong to you anymore. What am I?

Question #99

This is the only thing that gets broken without it being held or dropped. What is it?

Question #100

I thrive on food that you give me, but if you make me drink water, I die. What am I?

Level 2: Riddles #101 – 200

Question #101

What is the most boring chemical element?

Question #102

Which period of time weighs the least?

Question #103

Nickel and neon combine to form a number. Which one?

Question #104

What is equal to $k + 7k + 3k$?

Question #105

What do the following have that smoke does not have: cinders, fires, embers, and charcoal?

Question #106

I'm there close to you most of the time except maybe in the dark. I copy everything you do. What am I?

Question #107

This thing has one foot, no legs, and carries its house around. What is it?

Question #108

This storm is always rushing about. Which one?

Question #109

A well-dressed lady is on a bicycle and a badly dressed lady is on a unicycle. What is the difference between them?

Question #110

Spell hard water using only three letters.

Question #111

I exist in life but never in death. It's not possible to have fun without me. What am I?

Question #112

You just have to say my name and I cease to exist. What am I?

Question #113

_____ is needed for hardbound books as well as to stand up for your principles. Fill in the blank.

Question #114

This word describes the final punch in a boxing bout as well as a beautiful woman. Find the word.

Question #115

We are two sisters who live on opposite sides of the road. We work very well together. In fact, things are not clear if even one of us doesn't work correctly and yet we sisters never meet with each other. Who are we?

Question #116

A woman comes out of her house, which has all the doors facing north. She sees a bird outside her house that is walking by. Which bird is it?

Question #117

When a stone is put inside water it becomes a _____. Fill in the blank.

Question #118

This item gets better as it ages. In fact, it reaches the best stage when it stops breathing. And most people love it. What is it?

Question #119

Which person can sit on a baby and yet does not hurt the baby?

Question #120

I am not a common animal. I live in a few rainforests. I have an odd number of toes. People usually connect my name with laziness. What am I?

Question #121

With a hundred legs none of which help me stand straight, a long neck, and with no head, I am an item that keeps your home clean. What am I?

Question #122

Which is the weighty currency?

Question #123

This round thing is a sphere but not a ball. It holds all people, land, and water. What is it?

Question #124

If you lose this, it is likely that others around you will also lose theirs. What is this?

Question #125

Coming in different colors but am usually straight and erect, I have a dark-colored head and leave marks everywhere I go. What am I?

Question #126

A person was 20 years old in 1995 and was 25 years in 1990. Is this possible? If yes, how?

Question #127

I can move around when I am filled but stay still when I'm empty. What am I?

Question #128

Adrianne's mom has 3 daughters: April, May, and _____?

Question #129

I'm similar to a pancake though I'm crispier. But I'm usually square filled with smaller squares. What am I?

Question #130

I have a natural tuxedo and I don't walk. Instead, I march. What am I?

Question #131

Backward I'm not, but forward I'm heavy. What am I?

Question #132

How many kinds of animals did Moses take with him in the Ark?

Question #133

What old invention allows you to see through a wall?

Question #134

This man has married many women, but he himself has remained unmarried. Who is the man?

Question #135

Light as air but impossible to hold for more than a few seconds though some powerful people can hold it for a couple of minutes, what is it?

Question #136

What are the two things you can never have for breakfast?

Question #137

This thing tastes better than it smells. What is it?

Question #138

What is it that has a head at night and loses it in the morning?

Question #139

What is usually dark colored when it enters the water and red when it comes out of water?

Question #140

It is quite easy to catch this but impossible to throw. What is it?

Question #141

There are two peculiar siblings; one sibling is born from the other who in turn gives birth to the first. Which two siblings are we talking about?

Question #142

Which is the month that most people sleep the least in?

Question #143

Which building has the most number of stories?

Question #144

Mrs. Alex has two children. Her eldest is a daughter. What are the chances that the second one is a daughter too?

Question #145

Linda gets under the shower but doesn't get wet? How is this possible?

Question #146

What remains in the same place even when it goes off?

Question #147

Ring-a, ring-a roses; can you spell that without any R's?

Question #148

I have no fingers and still can point. I have no legs and still can run. I have no arms and still can strike. What am I?

Question #149

This thing is sticky and brown. What is it?

Question #150

No matter how bad things are in the Arctic, the people there will never eat a penguin? Why is that?

Question #151

This set has 30 men and only two women who hold all the power. Dressed in black and white, they can fight for hours on end. Who are they?

Question #152

The two ends of a 10-ft rope are nailed on to a wall. The middle of the rope dipping down is 5 feet from each end of the rope. How far are the ends of the rope from each other?

Question #153

If pirates were allowed to join the military, which service will they join?

Question #154

Why is it that you find what you are searching for in the last place?

Question #155

This has to be broken before you can use it. What is it?

Question #156

A horseman rode into town on Friday, stayed for three days, and again rode out on Friday. How is this possible?

Question #157

A man can go without any sleep for 10 days. Is it possible?

Question #158

This actually belongs to you. But, others use it far, far more than you do. What is it?

Question #159

Dolly's mom had 3 kids; April, May, and_____. Fill in the blank.

Question #160

A man claimed he found an old coin and declared it to be an antique piece because it had 150 BC inscribed on it. He wanted to sell the coin for a huge amount. This man is a fraud. How can you tell?

Question #161

What has 3 feet yet cannot walk?

Question #162

How many months of the year have 28 days?

Question #163

This has a mouth but never eats, has a bed but never sleeps, murmurs sometimes but never talks, runs but never walks. What is this?

Question #164

This is full of holes but can hold a lot of water. What is it?

Question #165

The first part of the name of this insect is another insect. Identify both the insects.

Question #166

A few people are walking in a straight line. There are two in front, two at the back and one in the middle. How many people are walking?

Question #167

You will find me at the start of eternity right until the beginning of the end. I start everything as well. What am I?

Question #168

Find the next letter in the sequence o, t, t, f, f, s, s, e, ____.

Question #169

A 5-letter word becomes shorter when you add two letters to it. Identify the 5-letter word.

Question #170

I'm that place where yesterday comes after today and tomorrow comes in the middle of the two. Where is this place?

Question #171

A truck driver and a pediatrician both love the same girl. When the truck driver had to go on a 10-day trip, he gave her 10 apples. Why?

Question #172

I tax people's brains and stump them many times. But when people get me, they are usually very happy. What am I?

Question #173

A girl was approached by an old lady and given this challenge. The old lady said, "If I write your exact age on this paper, you will have to give me $100, else I will." The girl was confident the old lady whom she has never met before will not guess her guess her right age and so she agreed to the challenge. The old lady wrote something on the paper and the girl read it and accepted defeat and gave the money to the old lady. What was on the paper?

Question #174

I get answered but I never question. What am I?

Question #175

A man buys a beautiful car for $10,000 without paying a dime. How is this possible?

Question #176

The more I become, the less you see me. What am I?

Question #177

Every dawn and dusk begins with me. Daisies unfold from me. I end all cold. Midday is centered upon me. Yet I'm not in the sun but am there in each day. What am I?

Question #178

This thing has no head but has a neck. Its neck sometimes forms a kind of a hurdle. What is it?

Question #179

This little boy buried his flashlight. Why did he do it?

Question #180

Which letter in the alphabet has the most amount of water in it?

Question #181

This place starts with a P and ends with an E and has thousands of letters. Which place?

Question #182

Why would someone living in Austin not be buried in New York?

Question #183

If everyone in a country bought a white car, what will we have?

Question #184

John throws a ball really, really hard. Yet it comes back to him even when no one touched it. How?

Question #185

An electric train was traveling in the northern direction and the wind was blowing in the southeastern direction. Which direction will the smoke go in?

Question #186

You have a page, which is empty except for a vertical line in the middle of it. Without touching the line, how can you make it longer?

Question #187

Complete this sequence of letters; JFMAMJJASON____.

Question #188

John and David are brothers working at different places and returning home to Austin for Christmas. John is coming from London, and David is coming from Prague. John's airplane is traveling at a speed of 550 mph and David's flight was traveling at 575 mph. The two planes meet at New York. Is John or David closer to home?

Question #189

I am in a strange situation. I have added 5 to 9, and the result is 2. And it is correct. How?

Question #190

John has no siblings; he's an only child. However, this man's father is John's father's son. Who is this man?

Question #191

Megan drives her car to the bank and screams, 'I'm bankrupt.' Why?

Question #192

There are 15 oranges in a basket to be shared among 15 boys and girls. Every child must get one orange and yet, one orange must be left in the basket at the end. How is this possible?

Question #193

A poor farmer takes some potatoes and peas to the market to sell. He has only one bag to carry both the vegetables. He puts the peas at the bottom of the bag and ties a knot to secure it. Then, he put the potatoes on the top part of the bag and ties another knot around it to secure it as well. When he reaches the market, a man comes to him to buy only the peas. The buyer has his own bag. How can the farmer transfer the peas from the bottom side of his bag to the buyer's bag without cutting the bag, without placing the vegetables anywhere on the ground or without trading and exchanging bags?

Question #194

Two sisters were born to the same mother in the same year, on the same day, and at the same time. Yet, these two are not twins. How is this possible?

Question #195

A ladder is hanging over a ship that is docked at the harbor. The ladder is 20 feet in length and has 20 rungs at a distance of 1 foot from each other. As of now, the 20th rung is just touching the water. A tide is coming on, and the water is rising at the rate of 6 inches every hour. How long before the 5th rung of the ladder will touch the water?

Question #196

Can a lady be taken to court if she's chooses to marry her widower's brother?

Question #197

There are three bulbs for the room upstairs and the switches for these bulbs are on the ground floor. You should identify each of the switches to the correct bulb it operates. You are allowed to climb up the stairs only once. But, you can turn on/off the switches any number of times. How will you identify the switches correctly?

Question #198

The king of a particular kingdom always thought things differently and out of the box. He was ill and had to decide which of his two sons should be placed on the throne after him. He decides to test their skills. He gave each of his sons a horse and told them to run a race. The horse that comes second will be his heir. The sons are quite puzzled at their father's request. However, they accept it and begin their race.

As expected, both the sons ride as slowly as possible to take the second place. After a while, the boys get quite frustrated with the exercise. At that time, they see a wise old sage meditating under a tree and decide to go to him for advice. The sage heard their problem and gave them a great solution. Both the boys agreed, got on to the horses, and raced back to the palace. What was the sage's solution?

Question #199

A lady lives on the 10th floor of a big apartment complex. She went to work every morning and returned in the evening, sometimes, late at night. Here was her daily routine:

- On her way down, she would always use the elevator right up to the ground floor
- On her way up, unless it was raining or she was traveling with others in the elevator, she would always go until the 6th floor, and then climb the balance four floor to her 10th-floor apartment

Why was she doing this?

Question #200

You and your friends are playing ping-pong and suddenly, out of the blue, someone hits the ping-pong ball in such a way that it gets stuck in the middle of a steel pipe whose mouth is open. You have your racket, your shoes, and laces, and bottles of water. How will you remove the ping-pong ball stuck in the steel pipe?

Level 3: Riddles #201 – 300

Question #201

A dashing cowboy hangs his hat, blindfolds himself, and shoots the hat with such accuracy that all the bullets make holes in it. His blindfold is perfectly in order, and there is nothing hanky-panky about it. The cowboy, though dashing, wasn't a great shot. Then, how does he manage this trick?

Question #202

A rapidly-growing water hyacinth plant is placed in the middle of a completely empty lake on Day 1. This plant becomes two on Day 2, and each of the two plants double in one day, and this goes on until on Day 24, half the lake is completely covered with water hyacinth plants. How long before the lake is completely covered?

Question #203

I am yellow in color and have a very sunny glow. I am fixed to the ground and **yet follow my king right around**. What am I?

Question #204

These two sisters live and work together in tandem. If something happens to one of them, the other is quite useless. Which pair of sisters are we talking about?

Question #205

I have a silver-colored liquid in a little case at the bottom, and the higher this liquid rises, the hotter it is. What am I?

Question #206

The only anagram of the word 'trinket' is someone who handles woolly things. What is the anagram?

Question #207

Whether there is rain or shine, I always meander all over town including your home, but I have never stepped into your home. What am I?

Question #208

These arrows from the sky come down heavily sometimes and light other times. We need them for our life. Yet, they can wreak havoc if the intensity of these arrows are very strong. What are these arrows?

Question #209

My lifespan is usually a few hours. I last longer if I am thick and die faster if I am thin. A single breath is all that is needed to kill me. What am I?

Question #210

This courageous goose fights with snakes and many times comes out as the winner. Which goose am I talking about?

Question #211

I am a parent, but I do not give birth and I do not nurse my children. I am rarely still and yet I cannot move. Without me, human life is very difficult. What am I?

Question #212

Full of teeth, this thing can never bite or eat! It is usually made with bone, metal, or plastic. What is it?

Question #213

Although I look light and I float harmlessly, I can cause a lot of destruction if you dash against me. I show only a very small part of me, and the rest of me is hidden deep within. What am I?

Question #214

Little Johnny was looking out of his home near the seashore and watched as a ship sank down into the sea. There was no storm, no typhoon, or anything else to drown the ship. And still, it went down. What do you think was actually happening?

Question #215

I am one of the most loyal friends you can ever have. Yes, many times, I show you my tongue. But, I am never rude or nasty to you and am ready to do anything for you. Who am I?

Question #216

This item comes in different colors though black or white is the most preferred one. It takes us all to a place where we have to go, but it can never bring us back. What is it?

Question #217

Sometimes, I have long tines, and at other times, I have short tines. But, my sound report is given long after my tines end. What am I?

Question #218

I can run and make you so irritated you can almost scream in frustrating. Yet, I never move from my place. I run so much that others can sometimes catch me and sometimes cannot catch me. What am I?

Question #219

This particular vegetable is dangerous for boats and ships. Which vegetable?

Question #220

I am filled with puzzles and problems. People either love me or hate me. I can run to infinity on either sides of a line. Some people find solutions to some of my problems. Still, there are infinite things to be found out about me. What am I?

Question #221

These two things are rarely seen together. Most of the times, they come separately; one bringing joy and the other sorrow. When they do meet on these very, very rare occasions, it is only to tell you that you are passing some of the best moments of your life. What is this pair?

Question #222

With no wings to help me, I can still soar and fly to the most distant lands in every part of the world or even universe. I can be gentle and happy or wild and crazy. Sometimes, I can scare even the most powerful men on earth? What am I?

Question #223

These things are usually filled up during the day, and nearly always empty at night. They come in pairs. What are they?

Question #224

People think I am more powerful than a gun or a sword. And yet, I am available at your local store at very cheap prices. What am I?

Question #225

This is one of the yummiest things anyone could have eaten and comes with a lot of different toppings. But, it can no middle, no beginning, and no end. What is it?

Question #226

I come in a mind-boggling variety of colors and shades. You will find me everywhere inside your house. Look at the ceiling or walls of your room, and you will see me. The only hitch is that I have to be wet if you want to put me on. What am I?

Question #227

This thing is round and goes deep into the earth. It is so deep that nothing can really put it up after it is made. However, there is something really soothing at the bottom that all of us need. What is this thing?

Question #228

I am made of wood and metal. I can be small or big. I have no feet, but my belly is full! My favorite place is the water. What am I?

Question #229

With the power to get rid of cold and gloom, this thing blooms and fumes when provoked. It can give you warmth but when in uncontrollable measure, can cause destruction. What is it?

Question #230

This is the only vegetable that is never frozen. It is always sold in its fresh form. Which vegetable?

Question #231

Find this thing that has 'kst' in its center, 'and' at the end, and 'in' in the beginning.

Question #232

I love it when you plunge in the knife to my heart and twist and turn that it can hurt. But even then, I open my heart to you. What am I?

Question #233

Identify the name of a great king using the following clues: His name starts and finishes with 500 and 5 is in the center. The first alphabet and the first number occupy the two sides of the center.

Question #234

Identify the number that looks like a pair of spectacles. If you finish writing it on a piece of paper, you cannot find the beginning or the end.

Question #235

You must endeavor to keep me straight and erect. However, typically, I am kept slightly bent or curved. When you are feeling sad, usually I bend further down. The risk is that if you bend me for too long, then it is possible that I cannot be straightened out again. What am I?

Question #236

Identify the thing that is not white from this list: The White House, golf balls, polar bears, marshmallows, milk, or white onions.

Question #237

My home is the tree and yet I have never been inside. If I fell off from the tree, I will surely die. What am I?

Question #238

Jerry was invited to a party that was filled with people. Yet, there was not a single person there. How is this possible?

Question #239

This sport can also be eaten. Which one?

Question #240

People of this nationality never fail to complete a marathon. Which nationality?

Question #241

Identify a unique thing about this set of words: Civic, Madam, Level, and Eye

Question #242

How can you convert half of five to four?

Question #243

Presently I have no eyes, but there was a time I did see. I also had thoughts then. But, now I am white and empty. What am I?

Question #244

What breaks but is never known to fall, and what falls but never known to break?

Question #245

What mostly comes in black-and-white and is red everywhere?

Question #246

Tom has 10 apples, and you take away three from him. How many do you have?

Question #247

The Mother Hen left her three little chicks in their round hut and went to pick up some groceries. She made breakfast and warned her chicks not to touch the food until she returned. But, when she came back from her shopping, she found the food was missing. Nobody else could have come inside because Mother Hen locked her hut from the outside. Now, look at the explanations given by the three chicks and identify the culprit from the lie that was being said:

- Chick #1: I was listening to the radio
- Chick #2: I was drawing
- Chick #3: I was reading my book in the corner

Question #248

This letter of the alphabet can fly, sing, and sting. Which one?

Question #249

A farmer has 450 sheep scattered all around the farm. He took just one shot, and he got them all together. How could he have done it?

Question #250

If 21=9, 9=4, 22=9, 8=5, 100=7, and 1000 = 8, then what is 16 equal to?

Question #251

My uncle is a goldsmith who is 6-ft and 2 inches tall. He is always eating. Can you imagine what he weighs?

Question #252

How many numbers from 1 to 100 have the letter A in their names?

Question #253

Do you how many sides a circle has?

Question #254

A man and his son were in a tragic car accident where the man died and the son was rushed to the hospital for an emergency surgery. The surgeon saw the boy and said, "I can't operate on him. He is my son!" How is this possible?

Question #255

Mr. Adam's peacock laid eggs in Mr. Smith's backyard. Now, Mr. Smith is claiming the eggs are his because they were laid in his backyard, and Mr. Adam says the eggs are his because the eggs were laid by his peacock. Who should you support?

Question #256

A plane crashed in the area between Mexico and US, and there was a big fight about where the survivors should be buried; in Mexico or US. Whose side are you on?

Question #257

General Gerald was surrounded by Indians as his entire army was wiped out in the battle. Suddenly, he spied a lamp fallen near him. He picks it up and rubs it, and out popped a genie. The genie said that the general can ask for three wishes, but whatever he wishes for, the Indians will get double of the same. So, if he wished for a gun, the Indians will get two guns, and so forth. The general thought for a while and made his wishes escaping death. What did he wish for himself?

Question #258

A nurse and a doctor have a baby boy. Yet the doctor is not the father and the mother is not the nurse of the baby. Is this possible at all? If yes, how?

Question #259

There are 12 kids in a room; 6 of them are wearing socks, 4 are wearing shoes, and 3 are wearing both shoes and socks. How many of the 12 kids are barefoot?

Question #260

This item can bring tears without the attached sorrow and make its journey towards the sky. Which is this item?

Question #261

What sits when it stands and jumps when it walks?

Question #262

The letter T and an island have something in common. Can you find the common thing?

Question #263

A man got a telephone call with some information while he was working the night shift. He rushed home and his informant was correct. He found his wife with a complete stranger he had never laid eyes on before. However, instead of being angry, he hugged her in joy and brought her breakfast in bed. What had actually happened?

Question #264

A snake charmer has 27 snakes and four cages. He has to use up all the cages, and he must have an odd number of snakes in each cage. How can he get this done?

Question #265

What is the best place in a train for a claustrophobic person to sit so that he spends the least time in a tunnel?

Question #266

What is the middle of nowhere?

Question #267

A farmer has 20 rabbits, 10 pigs, and 5 horses. If we assume that pigs are horses and rabbits are pigs, how many rabbits, horses, and pigs does the farmer have?

Question #268

Mr. and Mrs. John went on a romantic trip to the mountains for a week. However, Mrs. John returned home alone after 2 days and went to the police saying that her husband fell over the cliff and died. The next day, the detective in charge of the case came and arrested Mrs. John for the murder of her husband. The surprised lady confessed to her guilt but wanted to know how the detective found out the truth. He said all he needed to do was to call the travel agent who booked the trip for the couple. What information from the travel agent helped the detective solve the mystery?

Question #269

Mr. Jack called his daughter, Alexa, from his office and told her to buy some things from the grocery store. He told her that she will find money in an envelope on his desk. She looked at the envelope and saw that 98 was written on it. She went to the shop and bought various items for $90 so that she will have $8 left over. However, when she took out the money from the envelope, Alexa realized that she not only did not have any leftover money but was also short by $4. How did this happen?

Question #270

Where do the rich fish keep all their money?

Question #271

A lady has 7 children and half of them are girls. Is this possible? If yes, on what condition?

Question #272

A boy was ten on his last birthday and is going to be twelve on his next birthday. How can this be possible?

Question #273

There are two mothers, two daughters, one granddaughter, and one grandmother. What is the minimum number of people in this group?

Question #274

There are 25 men in a room sitting in such a way that each of them can see everything and everyone else in the room. Now, you must place an apple in such a way that all except one person should be able to see it. Where will you place this apple?

Question #275

A bullock travels a certain distance every day. Interestingly, one pair of its legs travel 25 miles while another pair travel about 26 miles each day. The bullock is perfectly normal and there is no magic involved. In what kind of situation is this possible?

Question #276

Two boys ordered iced tea. One of the boys drank the tea really fast while the other took a very long time to finish his drink. The one who drank slowly died whereas the one who drank fast survived. The glasses were examined and it was found that both the glasses were poisoned. How is it possible for the boy who drank the iced tea fast to have survived?

Question #277

The delivery man had to drop an important letter through the slot of the front door of Mr. Jackson. However, he noticed that a vicious dog with bared fangs was tied to a tree with a chain that was just long enough to reach the front door. The delivery man was a clever one. How did he outwit the dog?

Question #278

A little girl jumped off from a 100-foot ladder and yet did not get hurt except for a light scraping on her knees. How is this possible?

Question #279

A lady was walking along the railway track and suddenly spied an express train coming at a great speed toward her. She had to quickly jump off from the railway track. Yet, before she jumped off, the lady ran about 10 feet toward the train and then, jumped to safety. Why did she do this?

Question #280

Two men were found lying in the desert. One of them was alive and the other was dead. Both of the men were carrying the same kind of backpacks. The dead man's backpack was closed and the man who was alive had his backpack open. What was in the backpacks?

Question #281

You are horseback riding. To your right is a cliff and to your left is an elephant that is going at the same speed as your horse. A lion running behind you is coming at you again at the same speed as your horse, and there a hippo running by your side too. How can you save yourself from this situation?

Question #282

You are driving your car at 85 mph on a mountainous road with mountains on one side and a deep valley on the other side. A car is speeding towards you on the right side and an old man is walking at a slow pace on your left side. What will you hit to ensure minimum damage?

Question #283

A girl wanted to marry only someone who could think and get out of a tricky situation with ease. She was rich and beautiful and there were four men vying for her attention. She gave them a test and told them that the one who clears this test will be the winner. She stood in the middle of a 25 by 25 foot room and placed four stools in the four corners for the suitors to stand. They were given nothing else to draw, pull, hold, or do anything. They only had their wits to use. Now, the test was to touch the girl who was standing in the middle. The suitors could not walk across the room either. One man thought of a brilliant idea and owned the hand of his sweetheart. What was the idea?

Question #284

Craig died at sea and Beulah died in the mountains. Everyone was thrilled at Craig's death. Why?

Question #285

A sundial has the least number of moving parts. Which timepiece has the most number of moving parts? (It is typically filled with sand)

Question #286

A reporter visited a mental asylum to understand how the doctors decide if a patient is insane or not. The chief doctor said that they ask the following question to the patient, "Suppose you had to empty a bathtub full of water by choosing one of a spoon, bucket, or mug, which would you choose?"

The chief doctor then asked the reporter his choice. The reporter said, "I would choose the bucket because it carries more water than a spoon or mug." The doctor immediately admitted the reporter also. Why?

Question #287

Once a man wanted to test the thinking abilities of his very intelligent son. He sends him with some money to the market and tells him to buy only one item with which the family can eat, the cows can be fed, something can be planted, and something we can drink. What did the intelligent son buy in the market?

Question #288

A competition was held to see who could hold 'this thing' for the longest period of time. The one who held it was a man with no hands and feet. What was 'this thing?'

Question #289

Can you stand physically behind your friend in such a way that he also stands physically behind you?

Question #290

A math teacher finished teaching his Grade Six students all about the Roman numerals. Now, he gave them a test. He told them to convert IX to 6 using only one stroke and without lifting the pen from the paper until completion of the stroke. How is this possible?

Question #291

The police discovered the body of a man who was shot while he was in his car. No powder marks on his clothing indicated that the shooter was outside the car. But the windows and the doors were all shut. The only bullet found was inside his body. How was he shot?

Question #292

A man was standing on one bank of a river, and his dog was standing on the other bank. When the man called out to his dog, it came through the river without getting wet at all. There was no bridge connecting the two banks. How could this have happened?

Question #293

In this game, the winners move backward, and the losers move forwards. Identify the game.

Question #294

What is the first thing that comes in an emergency, which you get to see only two times in a lifetime?

Question #295

You get in through one hole and emerge through three holes. When you are inside, you are all set to go out. But when you go out, you are still inside. What is this strange item?

Question #296

Today is Monday. Can you calculate what day of the week will be 61 days from today?

Question #297

You have been given a square cake with one of the corners cut. How will you cut the cake into two equal halves?

Question #298

A man takes five days to finish eating 100 apples by increasing 6 apples each day. Using this information, find out how many apples he would have eaten on Day 4?

Question #299

A landscaper has to place 4 trees in such a way that they are equidistant from each other. How can this be done?

Question #300

The cost of an apple is 40 cents, the cost of a grapefruit is 80 cents, and a banana costs 60 cents. With the same logic, how much will a pear cost?

Level 4: Riddles #300-350

Question #301

Look at the following equations:

$66 = 2$
$99 = 2$
$888 = 6$
$00 = 2$
$7777 = 0$
$667 = 2$
$267 = 1$
$823 = 2$

Using the same logic, what is 2876 equal to?

Question #302

Sometimes I can sharp, at other times I am dull. I can be big or small. I can be straight or curved. I can be simple or ornate. Although I can be very, very sharp, I cannot answer any questions. What am I?

Question #303

A car driver is going down the wrong side of the road in broad daylight. He passes through traffic inspectors and they don't penalize him. Why?

Question #304

It howls and cries without a voice. It flutters without wings. It bites without teeth, and mutters without a mouth. What is it?

Question #305

A wise man that had a successful business was going to retire. He wanted to choose the wisest among his three sons to take over the business. He gave them a test. He told them to get something from the market that can fill his entire room and yet fit into a small pocket too.

The first son bought some muslin cloth, which could fit into his pocket but could hardly cover one length of his father's room. The second had bought some hay, which he had struggled to fit into his pocket, but was barely enough to cover one side of the floor.

The third son came and what he bought pleased the father so much that he was made successor. What did the third son bring from the market?

Question #306

A genie appeared to a good man in his dream and said that for all the good work he has done, he will be rewarded with a wish. It can be anything, but it had to be one wish only. The genie gave the good man one day to think about it and said he will return the next night to grant the wish.

The good man woke up the next morning and told his wife and parents about his dream. His wife wanted a son because they had been childless for many years now. His blind mother wanted her eyesight, and his father wanted to be rich. The good man was clever too. He combined all the three wishes into one and asked the genie for one wish. What was it?

Question #307

A winemaker has 21 vintage wine barrels. Seven of these were empty, seven were full, and seven were half-full. He wanted to divide this set of barrels among his three sons such that each of them got exactly the same number of empty, half-full, and full barrels. How can he do this?

Question #308

A man who had recently bought a new house and was getting it all set up went to the hardware shop and asked the price of a particular item. The shopkeeper replied, '$1 for one.' The man paid $3 for 600. What was the item?

Question #309

This man does not have all his fingers on one hand. What would you call him?

Question #310

A lady was watching TV in her hotel room when she heard a knock on her door. She opened it to find a complete stranger standing outside her door. When he saw her, he immediately apologized to her say that he had mistaken this room to be his and went away. The lady locked the door and called the reception and informed them about this incident. Why was she suspicious of the man?

Question #311

You have one bag of coffee. Now, you must fit the coffee into two separate bags of the same size. How can you do this?

Question #312

Remember the Borgias who were infamous for murdering people with poison cleverly? Here is a riddle based on Lucia Borgias. She invited Duke Wellington, whom she wanted to get rid of, for lunch. Knowing the Borgias' ability to use poisons, the victim insisted that he would eat any food only after she had taken the first bite. Lucia Borgias readily agreed. After a hearty meal of venison and steamed vegetables that both of them shared exactly as per the Duke's conditions, it was time for fruits. There were figs and grapes, and one apple only in the fruit basket. Lucia took a knife and neatly cut the apple into two halves, ate one half and gave the other to the Duke. He took one bite of it, and after a minute keeled over backward quite dead from the poison in the apple. How did Lucia Borgias achieve this?

Question #313

A dog had three puppies, Tony, Sony, and Ronny. What is the mother's name.

Question #314

Four friends - Freddy, Martha, Sean, and Dean - need to escape to safety by crossing over a dark and dangerous river that is full of crocodiles. The only thing these animals are scared of is the light from a flashlight. There is a boat available to them and they have a flashlight, which can run for only 12 minutes more.

Freddy can row the boat and cross over in 1 minute, Martha can do it in 2 minutes, Sean can do it in 4 minutes, and Dean does it in 5 minutes. Only two people can go in the boat each time and that two rowing at the speed of the slower individual, and the flashlight has to be kept burning else the crocs will eat up the people on the boat. In what order should the four friends cross the river so that all can be safe?

Question #315

You have two little kittens, and you need to give away one. Yet, you want to keep both. How can you do it?

Question #316

Three engineers said that John was their brother. But, when asked, John said he had no brothers. Who is lying?

Question #317

The 22nd and the 24th Presidents of the US had the same parents and yet they were not brothers. There are no 'switching at birth' stories nor was one of them adopted. You already know that there were no women presidents yet so they couldn't be a sister-brother pair. So, then how is this possible?

Question #318

How can you place a pen on the floor such that no one can jump over it?

Question #319

A rich man had a dog, an antique piece of jewelry, and cash in his house. One day, a thief broke into the house and kidnapped the dog. The next day, the rich man reported the robbery to the police and said two items were missing even though only the dog was kidnapped. He was telling the truth. Can you explain how?

Question #320

Why do Chinese people consume far more rice than Japanese people even though both love rice equally?

Question #321

Two guards were standing outside their barracks on guard duty. One was facing down the road to see any approaching intruder from the south and the other was facing up the road watching for signs of danger coming from the north. Suddenly one guard said to the other, "Why is there a smile on your face?" How did he know that his colleague was smiling?

Question #322

You enter a little room with others too. The doors close and when the doors open again, you are in a different room. Magic? No, not at all. Can you think and explain the little room?

Question #323

A farmer was traveling back from the city after buying an untrained dog and two chickens for his farm. He had to cross a river on a boat that can hold only two people/animals at a time. If he left one chicken back with the dog, the chicken is bound to be eaten. How can he ensure that he takes all of them across the river safely?

Question #324

Jane made her coffee in the microwave every morning. She was mix her coffee and place it in the microwave for two minutes. When it was done, she would open the door and take her coffee. However, on some days before taking out her coffee from the microwave she would run it for another two seconds and then remove it. What was the need for the two seconds?

Question #325

In the medieval ages, a man from the village got his first job in the city. He has a problem waking up on time for his early morning shift, which starts at dawn. The first time he is late, his boss warns him that he repeated this late-coming one more time, he will fire him. The poor man goes back to his village and buys a rooster to wake him up on time. The next dawn shift, he is again late for work, and his boss fires him. Why was he late again despite the rooster crowing and waking him up?

Question #326

Jack's birthday was on December 29th. Yet, his birthday was always in summer. How is this possible?

Question #327

A lady walked to the billing counter with a book. The man at the counter looks at it and says, "That will be $5." The lady pays him the money and walks away without the book. The man at the counter also does not call her back. Explain.

Question #328

A hijacker on the plane, which was carrying 10 passengers and valuable cargo, demanded 11 parachutes from the crew. The crew gave all eleven to the hijacker. He wore one of the parachutes and jumped off the plane with the valuable cargo. Why did he ask for 11 when he needed only one?

Question #329

Gerald looked at the reflection of his face in the window on the 30th floor. Impulsively, he jumped across the window over to the other side. He landed safely without a single bruise. How can this be possible?

Question #330

There is a little island in the middle of a huge lake in a remote part of a cold country. There has never been a bridge that connected the island to the mainland across the lake. There are no boats or ships either . There is a tractor that goes around the island every day delivering hay to everyone.

How did the tractor get to the island in the first place? No, there is no tractor manufacturing plant on the island.

Question #331

A lady and her daughter was sitting in a coffee shop when an elderly gentleman walked in and sat down with them. Both the lady and her daughter said, "Hello, father!" How is this possible?

Question #332

This thing turns everything around, and yet remains stationary. What is this item?

Question #333

These things have rings but no fingers. Nowadays, they follow humans around wherever we go. What are these things?

Question #334

What is a five letter word that remains only one when two are moved?

Question #335

I can be thin or thick. The leaner I am, the cooler I look. I have many things inside me with which you can see many things outside me. What am I?

Question #336

A farmer constructed a square fence for his cows. You can count 27 poles on each side of the square fence. How many poles did he use totally?

Question #337

The head of a desert tribe died leaving 17 camels to be shared among this three sons as follows: the eldest son gets half the camels, the second son gets $1/3^{rd}$ of them, and the youngest son gets $1/9^{th}$ of them. The sons were perplexed. They sat on the wall of their home, morose and sad, not knowing how to get to ½ of 17 camels, $1/3^{rd}$ of 17 camels, and $1/9^{th}$ of 17 camels.

No one wanted to kill and share the meat of dead camels, right? A wise man with a camel passed by this house and saw the sad faces of the boys and asked for the reason. The eldest son explained their problem to the wise man and he gave a solution that they used to solve the problem. Do you know the solution?

Question #338

You have a 9l can and a 4l can at your disposal. There is no other measuring equipment or vessel available to you. You need to measure out 6 liters of water using these two cans only. You have access to unlimited water. How will you measure the required quantity?

Question #339

How can you ensure that your friend Bob has your correct phone number without actually divulging it? You cannot talk directly with him. But you can send a note to him through another person and make the content relevant so that you will know if Bob has your number or not. What is the thing you can write on that note?

Question #340

You have to visit your grandmother who lives at the edge of the forest. You have to cross 5 bridges and pay half of whatever you are carrying as toll tax. In return, the officials will give you back one full item of whatever you have paid. You have decided to take cake for your grandmother. How many cakes must you carry so that you can take exactly two cakes for your grandmother?

Question #341

If the time seen in the reflection of an analog clock is showing 2:30, what will be the correct time?

Question #342

What is that word in the dictionary that is right if pronounced wrong and wrong if pronounced right?

Question #343

Three types of oranges are mixed up in a closed basket. How many oranges must you pick up to ensure you get at least two types of oranges?

Question #344

In a school of 100 students, 55 chose theater and 44 chose music. 20 chose both. How many students chose neither theater nor music?

Question #345

A 100-ft ribbon needs to be cut into 1-ft strips. The time taken to cut one 1-ft strip is one second. How long before 100 1-ft strips are cut?

Question #346

When the clock in my living room struck 6 o'clock, I noticed that there was a 30-second interval between the 1st and the 6th stroke. How long will it take for the clock to strike twelve midnight?

Question #347

You purchase these items to eat, but you never eat them. What are these items?

Question #348

A chicken and a loaf of bread together cost John $1.06. The chicken costs $1 more than the loaf of bread. Find the cost of each item.

Question #349

The captain of a Japanese ship left his diamond ring and watch on his table and went for a bath. When he emerged 15 minutes later, he realized the valuables were missing. The ship was at sea and only one of the four crew members could have stolen them. The captain asked them what they were doing in the last 15 minutes and the replies were like this:

- The cook said he was getting meat from the freezer to prepare lunch

- The sailor said he was up at the mast setting the right flag which had turned upside down

- The radio officer said he was in the radio room sending a message to the company that the ship is going to reach the next port in 2 days' time

- The navigation officer said he was up all night and was sleeping in his cabin

The captain found the culprit because one of the above statements was a lie. Which one?

Question #350

There are three clocks in my house. One is running slowly, one is running fast, and one is keeping the correct time. The times on the three clocks read as 10:04, 9:54, and 10:12. Which is the correct time?

ANSWERS

Answers to Riddles #1-100

Answers 1 - 10

Answer #1: A funny bone

Answer #2: A table

Answer #3: A gymnast

Answer #4: A keyboard

Answer #5: The living room

Answer #6: Remove the S from SIX and you are left with IX, which is an odd number (9 in Roman numerals)

Answer #7: A mailman

Answer #8: The Dead Sea

Answer #9: Watermelon

Answer #10: An actor or actress

Answers 11 - 20

Answer #11: A rainbow

Answer #12: Blood

Answer #13: Soap

Answer #14: A teacher

Answer #15: A fence

Answer #16: Because they preferred apples to dates

Answer #17: Mother Earth

Answer #18: A jersey

Answer #19: Blood tests

Answer #20: Emojis

Answers 21 - 30

Answer #21: A skeleton

Answer #22: Kiwi

Answer #23: A bank

Answer #24: A pilot

Answer #25: A coffin break

Answer #26: Frisbee

Answer #27: Staircase

Answer #28: Piano

Answer #29: Clock

Answer #30: Because they have so many fans

Answers 31 - 40

Answer #31: 3

Answer #32: No staircase because it is a one-floor home

Answer #33: Their friend Friday

Answer #34: 666+66+6+6+6=750

Answer #35: Because the three people who went were the grandfather, father, and son

Answer #36: Tectonic plate

Answer #37: Starting, staring, string, sting, sing, sin, in, I

Answer #38: Smoke or Air

Answer #39: A bat

Answer #40: Footsteps

Answers 41 - 50

Answer #41: Corn

Answer #42: Yesterday, today, and tomorrow

Answer #43: Timetables, multiplication tables, the periodic table

Answer #44: Milk

Answer #45: Mushroom

Answer #46: Orange

Answer #47: A home full of gadgets

Answer #48: Diamonds

Answer #49: A penny

Answer #50: A stamp

Answers 51 - 60

Answer #51: SWIMS

Answer #52: The letter M

Answer #53: The word 'incorrectly'

Answer #54: Hard boil it and drop it on something thick and soft

Answer #55: A ruler

Answer #56: The eldest son because on Christmas morning in New York there would have been snow!

Answer #57: A lie

Answer #58: Later

Answer #59: Shadow

Answer #60: Neutron

Answers 61 - 70

Answer #61: Lead

Answer #62: Both weigh the same - 1 pound

Answer #63: Krypton

Answer #64: Helium (he) and aluminum (al)

Answer #65: Rectangle because it has the most letters

Answer #66: By burning candles or incense with their scent

Answer #67: Chocolate

Answer #68: Onion

Answer #69: Lightbulb

Answer #70: Because then it would be your foot

Answers 71 - 80

Answer #71: Yellow paint

Answer #72: Quack-ers

Answer #73: Palm

Answer #74: A potato.

Answer #75: Your left hand

Answer #76: Catfish

Answer #77: Barber

Answer #78: Because the engineer was the girl's father

Answer #79: Don't be scared because I've got you completely covered

Answer #80: Beauty, because as a proverb goes, beauty lies in the eyes of the bee-holder

Answers 81 - 90

Answer #81: A coat of paint

Answer #82: Because the man shot his reflection

Answer #83: Gravity

Answer #84: A rooster doesn't lay eggs!

Answer #85: She came to the place of the crime without being told the location

Answer #86: Simple - stop imagining

Answer #87: An anchor

Answer #88: Because the helicopter was on the ground

Answer #89: Because the third guy is bald!

Answer #90: A coffin

Answers 91 - 100

Answer #91: A candle

Answer #92: A clock

Answer #93: A needle

Answer #94: Paper

Answer #95: A towel

Answer #96: Human being; we crawl as a baby, walk on two legs when we are young adults and need a crutch (three legs) when we are old

Answer #97: They both weigh meat because they work in a butcher's shop

Answer #98: Secret

Answer #99: A promise

Answer #100: Fire

Answers to Riddles #101-200

Answers 101 - 110

Answer #101: Boron

Answer #102: A light year

Answer #103: Nine. Ni (nickel) and ne (neon)

Answer #104: 11000 - K is a symbol for 1000

Answer #105: The letter R

Answer #106: Your shadow

Answer #107: A snail

Answer #108: Hurricane

Answer #109: Attire

Answer #110: ICE

Answers 111 - 120

Answer #111: The letter 'f'

Answer #112: Silence

Answer #113: Spine

Answer #114: Knockout

Answer #115: A pair of eyes

Answer #116: Penguin; she lives at the South Pole

Answer #117: Whetstone

Answer #118: Wine

Answer #119: Babysitter

Answer #120: Sloth

Answers 121 - 130

Answer #121: A broom

Answer #122: Pound

Answer #123: Earth

Answer #124: Temper

Answer #125: Pencil

Answer #126: Yes, the person was born in 2015 BC (Before Christ), which goes in the reverse order. So, 20 years after 2015 BC would have been 1995 and 25 years after would have been 1990

Answer #127: Glove

Answer #128: Adrianne

Answer #129: Waffles

Answer #130: Penguin

Answers 131 - 140

Answer #131: Ton – not

Answer #132: None, it was Noah not Moses who took animals in the Ark

Answer #133: A window

Answer #134: A priest

Answer #135: Breath

Answer #136: Lunch and dinner

Answer #137: Tongue

Answer #138: A pillow

Answer #139: Lobster, when it is cooked in water

Answer #140: A cold

Answers 141 - 150

Answer #141: Day and night

Answer #142: February because it has the least number of nights

Answer #143: A library

Answer #144: 50% - the chances of the gender of the second child is independent of the gender of the first child

Answer #145: Because she doesn't turn on the water

Answer #146: An alarm clock

Answer #147: T-H-A-T

Answer #148: Clock

Answer #149: A stick

Answer #150: Because penguins live in Antarctica

Answers 151 - 160

Answer #151: Chess pieces

Answer #152: The ends are nailed together

Answer #153: The Navy - because they love to sail

Answer #154: Because after you find it you stop looking

Answer #155: An egg

Answer #156: The name of his horse was Friday

Answer #157: Yes, he can sleep at night

Answer #158: Your name

Answer #159: Dolly

Answer #160: BC means before Christ and the concept of BC did not exist until after Christ was born

Answers 161 - 170

Answer #161: A yardstick

Answer #162: All 12 months

Answer #163: A river

Answer #164: A sponge

Answer #165: Bee, beetle

Answer #166: Three

Answer #167: The letter E

Answer #168: N - The first letter of number names 1-9

Answer #169: Short

Answer #170: A dictionary

Answers 171 - 180

Answer #171: Because an apple a day keeps the doctor away

Answer #172: A riddle

Answer #173: "Your exact age"

Answer #174: The telephone

Answer #175: When he pays $10,000 he doesn't have to add a dime.

Answer #176: Darkness

Answer #177: The letter D

Answer #178: Bottle

Answer #179: Because the batteries died

Answer #180: C

Answers 181 – 190

Answer #181: Post office

Answer #182: Because he is still living

Answer #183: A white carnation

Answer #184: Because he threw it up

Answer #185: An electric train will not emit smoke

Answer #186: By simply drawing a line shorter line next to it

Answer #187: D; the first letters of the months of the year

Answer #188: Both are at the same distance from home (Austin) because now they are both in New York.

Answer #189: It is 9 am. I add 4 hours to it, and I get 2 pm.

Answer #190: John himself

Answers 191 - 200

Answer #191: Because she is playing Monopoly

Answer #192: Give one orange each to 14 of the children and give the last orange still in the basket to the 15th child

Answer #193: He first transfers the potatoes to the buyer's bag and secures it tightly with a knot. He then turns the bag inside out and fills the space with the peas, and secures it with another tight knot. Now, the farmer reverses the sides of the bag again and transfers the potatoes back to his bag.

Answer #194: The two girls were two of triplets born to the mother

Answer #195: This will never happen because as the tide rises, the ship and the overhanging ladder will also rise

Answer #196: If her husband is a widower, then she is dead, and this question has no meaning

Answer #197: Put on switch#1 and it for a few minutes. Then, put off switch #1, and put on switch #2. Now, quickly climb the stairs and you will see the bulb connected to switch #2 is on, and therefore, easy to identify. Carefully, touch the other two bulbs. The warm one (because it was just switched off) will be switch #1 and the cold one will be switch #3

Answer #198: The sage told the boys to exchange their horses, and then, both of them tried to race the other to come first!

Answer #199: The lady was just tall enough to reach up to the button for floor #6. The ground floor button was never a problem. On her way up, if she had others with her in the elevator, she would ask one of them to press floor #10, or if it was raining, she would have an umbrella, which she used to press floor #10. On other days, she would press floor #6, get off, and walk the rest of the way!

Answer #200: Pour water into the steel pipe and watch the ball come up to the surface!

Answers to Riddles #201-300

Answers 201 - 210

Answer #201: Simple. He hangs the hat on his gun!

Answer #202: On Day 25, because all the plants double and use the double the space!

Answer #203: A sunflower

Answer #204: A pair of scissors

Answer #205: A mercury thermometer

Answer #206: Knitter

Answer #207: The streets

Answer #208: The rains

Answer #209: A candle

Answer #210: Mongoose

Answers 211 - 220

Answer #212: A tree

Answer #213: A comb

Answer #214: An iceberg

Answer #21: The captain of a submarine was slowly taking his ship down into the water where it belongs

Answer #218: A dog

Answer #216: A coffin

Answer #217: Lightning

Answer #218: A running nose

Answer #219: A leek (or leak)

Answer #220: Mathematics

Answers 221 - 230

Answer #221: Smiles and tears

Answer #222: Human imagination

Answer #223: Shoes

Answer #224: A pen

Answer #225: A doughnut

Answer #226: Paint

Answer #227: A well of water

Answer #228: A ship

Answer #229: A flame of fire

Answer #230: Lettuce

Answers 231 - 240

Answer #231: Inkstand

Answer #232: A lock

Answer #233: King DAVID

Answer #234: 8

Answer #235: Your back

Answer #236: Polar bears; their fur is colorless and transparent and free from pigment. If reflects light which makes polar bears appear white

Answer #237: Leaves

Answer #238: Because everyone was married

Answer #239: Squash

Answer #240: The Finnish

Answers 241 - 250

Answer #241: They all spell the same forward and backward

Answer #242: From FIVE, take away F and E, and you are left with IV, which is 4

Answer #243: A skull

Answer #244: Day and Night; day breaks and night falls

Answer #245: Newspaper (red to be seen as homonym of read)

Answer #246: Three, because you took away three from Tom

Answer #247: Chick #3 is lying because there are no corners in a round house

Answer #248: B (bee)

Answer #249: He used the panoramic view to shoot them from his camera

Answer #250: 16 = 7; because the equation is formed by counting the number of letters in the number name of the left hand side number and writing in number form on the right hand side; for example 100 (HUNDRED) has 7 letters; 1000 (THOUSAND) has 8 letters, and so forth

Answers 251 - 260

Answer #251: Gold, because he is a goldsmith

Answer #252: None

Answer #253: Two; inside and outside

Answer #254: Because the surgeon was the boy's mother

Answer #255: Neither; because peacocks don't lay eggs

Answer #256: I hope you are not on any one of the two sides because survivors ought not to be buried

Answer #257: One glass eye, one broken leg, and half-beaten to death

Answer #258: The nurse was the father and the doctor was the mother

Answer #259: 5 are barefooted; 3 are wearing both, therefore, people wearing only socks is 6-3 = 3, and 4-3 = 1 is wearing only shoes. The total number of kids who have something on their feet is 3 + 3 + 1 = 5. Therefore, kids who are barefoot are 12 − 7 = 5

Answer #260: Smoke

Answers 261 - 270

Answer #261: A kangaroo

Answer #262: They both are in the middle of water

Answer #263: His wife had given birth to their son!

Answer #264: He puts 9 snakes each in three cages and fits all the three cages into the fourth one.

Answer #265: He should sit at the last seat because the train will be accelerating as it enters the train and so he will spend the least time inside it

Answer #266: The letter H

Answer #267: 20 rabbits, 10 pigs, and 5 horses; our assumptions do not change facts

Answer #268: The travel agent said that Mrs. John booked two tickets for the onward journey but only one ticket for the return. So, obviously, she had planned to murder him and return alone.

Answer #269: Alexa had read the amount of money upside down; it was actually 86 and not 98

Answer #270: In the River Bank

Answers 271 - 280

Answer #271: Half of the 7 children can be daughters only if the rest of the kids are daughters too

Answer #272: It is possible if the boy's 11th birthday is today

Answer #273: Three; a grandmother with her daughter and her daughter

Answer #274: Place the apple on that one person's head

Answer #275: The bullock works on an oil mill and keeps moving in a circular clockwise direction. So, every day, the legs on the inner side of the circle travel lesser than the legs on the outer side of the circle.

Answer #276: The poison was in the ice. The ice melted slowly and infused into the drink. The boy who drank fast did not die because the ice was still frozen and the poison was not released into the drink. For the boy who drank slowly, however, the ice had melted and the poison was released into the drink.

Answer #277: He ran around the tree four times allowing the dog to chase him and each time, the chain got wrapped around the tree leaving the unwound part shorter than before. This prevented the dog to reach the front door after which the delivery man dropped the letter through the slot and went on his way, unharmed and free

Answer #278: The girl jumped from one of the lower rungs from the bottom which is why she didn't get hurt.

Answer #279: Because the lady was in a tunnel at the time she saw the express train speeding toward her. She was about 10 feet before the end of the tunnel. So, she ran 10 feet forward and then jumped off to safety well before the train could come anywhere near her.

Answer #280: Their parachutes; the men were skydiving, the dead man's pack did not open and he fell to his death. The other man's pack opened and he landed safely

Answers 281 - 290

Answer #281: Simply step down from the merry-go-round that you are on

Answer #282: Hit the car brake for minimum damage!

Answer #283: He asked the girl to walk across to him so that he could reach her and touch her!

Answer #284: Both were hurricanes and a hurricane that does at sea causes little or no harm

Answer #285: An hourglass

Answer #286: Wouldn't a sensible person pull the plug to empty a bathtub?

Answer #287: The son bought a big watermelon; the pulp to eat, the juice to drink, the rind for the cows, and the seeds to plant

Answer #288: Breath

Answer #289: Yes, by standing back to back

Answer #290: Just draw S before IX and you get SIX

Answers 291 - 300

Answer #291: The car was a convertible and the man was shot when the roof of the car was down

Answer #292: The dog was able to walk across the river because it was frozen

Answer #293: Tug of war

Answer #294: The letter E

Answer #295: A shirt

Answer #296: Saturday; each day of the week is repeated every 7 days; therefore, the 63rd day will be a Monday again; from here take away two, and you get Saturday

Answer #297: Cut the cake horizontally so that you get an equal top half and bottom half

Answer #298: 26 apples; he would have had to start with 8 apples on day 1, and then the progression is as follows: 8, 14, 20, 26, and 32

Answer #299: Place three trees at the corners of an equilateral triangle and place the 4th tree at the center of the three, which will result in the shape of a tetrahedron or a pyramid.

Answer #300: Pear will cost 40 cents; each vowel in the name of the fruit costs 20 cents

Answers to Riddles #301 – 350

Answers 301 - 310

Answer #301: 2876 = 3; each circle within a number is equal to 1; so, 6, 9, 0, has one circle each and 8 has 2 circles within it.

Answer #302: A knife

Answer #303: Because he was walking!

Answer #304: The wind

Answer #305: A match; the light from a lit match can easily fill the entire room, and it can easily be fit into any pocket

Answer #306: He said to the genie, "I want my mother to see my son playing in our large garden in a beautiful golden swing."

Answer #307: Use four of the 7 half-full barrels to get two fully barrels. Now, the winemaker will be left with 9 full barrels, 3 half-full barrels, and 9 empty barrels, which can be shared among the three sons.

Answer #308: The man bought three numbers 6, 0, and 0, which was his house number

Answer #309: A normal man because everyone does not have all their fingers on one hand

Answer #310: She was suspicious because if the man had thought it was his own room, he wouldn't knock. He would have tried to open the door with his key. He was probably a burglar hoping to break into an empty room. He was using the knock to check if the room was occupied or not.

Answers 311 - 320

Answer #311: Put the empty bags into each other and fill the two bags with coffee.

Answer #312: She coated one side of the knife (with which she was going to cut the apple into two halves) with the poison and carefully gave the poison-coated side of the fruit to the Duke.

Answer #313: What' is the name of the mother dog. Notice there is no question mark after the 'What is the mother's name.' It is a full stop and hence it is a sentence implying 'What' is the mother's name.

Answer #314: Here is the process that will help them reach to safety:

- Freddy and Martha will take 2 minutes to reach the other side where Martha will remain and Freddy will begin the return journey
- Freddy will return in 1 minute
- Sean and Dean will take the flashlight and complete the journey in 5 minutes
- Now, Martha will return with the flashlight in 2 minutes
- Then Freddy and Martha will cross the river in 2 minutes

So, the total time take is (2 + 1 + 5 + 2 + 2) = 12 minutes

Answer #315: Name the kitten you are going to keep back as 'both.'

Answer #316: All are telling the truth. The three engineers are John's sisters

Answer #317: The 22nd and the 24th Presidents were both the same person – Grover Cleveland

Answer #318: By placing the pen in a standing or slightly slanting position against the wall

Answer #319: The antique piece of jewelry was part of the dog's collar

Answer #320: Because there are far more Chinese people in the world than Japanese people

Answers 321 - 330

Answer #321: Because they were standing facing each other

Answer #322: The little room is an elevator

Answer #323: First, he takes the dog leaves it on the other side and returns. He then takes one of the chickens, and takes it to the other side, leaves it there, and brings back the dog with him. He then leaves the dog on this side of the river, and takes the second chicken and drops it with its brother. He then returns to take the dog back.

Answer #324: Sometimes, the handle of her coffee mug would be facing the other side making it difficult for her to remove it. That extra two seconds is enough to get the handle positioned conveniently for her to remove her coffee mug.

Answer #325: Because a rooster crows either just a few minutes before dawn or at the crack of dawn

Answer #326: Because Jack lived in Australia, which is in the southern hemisphere

Answer #327: The lady was returning an overdue book to the library

Answer #328: The hijacker only wanted the valuable cargo and he needed to let the crew members think he was going to take the 10 passengers as hostages so that they will not take the risk of giving any faulty parachute

Answer #329: Gerald was a window cleaner and he was jumping into the apartment and not out of the apartment

Answer #330: The tractor was brought during the winter season when the lake was completely frozen

Answers 331 - 340

Answer #331: Yes, the elderly gentleman was a priest

Answer #332: A mirror

Answer #333: Mobile phones

Answer #334: Any five letter word with 'one' in it; money, loner, stone, phone, etc

Answer #335: A television

Answer #336: 104 poles; remember that the corner poles are common to two sides; therefore, 25 poles * 4 sides + 4 corner poles = 104 poles

Answer #337: He added his camel to the 17 and now the sons had 18 camels. So, ½ of 18 is 9, 1/3 of 18 is 6, and 1/9 of 18 is 2, which resulted in 9 + 6 + 2 = 17 camels. The extra one was the old man's and he took it! The wise man was a mathematician too!

Answer #338: Fill the 9l can. Pour out 4 liters of water into the 4l can and throw it out. Pour out another 4 liters of water into the 4l can and throw out that too. Now, pour out the remaining 1 liter of water into the 4l can and keep it there. Again, fill the 9l can and pour out enough water to fill the 4l can (this will need only 3 liters of water to fill as there is already 1 liter in it). The amount remaining in the 9l can will be the required 6 liters of water

Answer #339: You can write a note asking him to call you at a specified time. If he calls you, he has your number, else he doesn't have your number

Answer #340: You need to take only two cakes to achieve this purpose; at each toll you will give half (one of two cakes) and they will return one cake to you and therefore at each toll, you will have both the cakes with you.

Answers 341 - 350

Answer #341: The correct time is 9:30

Answer #342: The word 'wrong'

Answer #343: As there are three types of oranges, picking up four oranges will ensure you get at least two types

Answer #344: 21 students chose neither; 20 students chose both means 55 − 20 = 35 students chose theater, and 44 − 20 = 24 chose music. Therefore, 100 − (20 + 35 + 24) = 21 students chose neither subject

Answer #345: 99 seconds because when the 99th 1-ft strip is cut, the 100th one is also ready and the extra second is not needed.

Answer #346: 66 seconds; at 6 o'clock, there are five intervals between the strokes which means each interval is 30/5 = 6 seconds. When the clock has to strike 12, there will be 11 intervals which translates to 11 * 6 = 66 seconds

Answer #347: Anything that is used for eating including plates, bowls, spoons, knives, forks, etc.

Answer #348: Cost of bread is $0.03 and the cost of chicken is $1.03

Answer #394: The seaman; the Japanese flag has only a red circle on a white background and it can never be upside down

Answer #350: The clock showing 10.04 is the right time; one is slow and the other is fast

Conclusion

So, did you have fun solving these riddles? How many did you get easily and how many frustrated you? I am sure you felt that unique sense of satisfaction when you got a correct answer, right? That is the power of riddles. They are fun, stimulating to the brain, and extraordinarily satisfying.

Solving riddles is far more fun than merely doing assignments and homework or learning for a test. Riddles offer a wholesome entertainment option that involves children, parents, grandparents, uncles, aunts, cousins, neighbors, and everyone else who loves to use their brains and get cleverer than before. So, go ahead and have fun playing with your children, your entire family, and friends. And if you are stuck, you can always take a peek into the answer section!

Recommended Books

It's been said that questions are signs of an active mind, which is crucial for children growing up to be intelligent, smart, and wise adults. Riddles are one of the best - and fun - ways of stimulating the mind so that it continues to become better and smarter.

Our fun quiz challenges in this book are extracted from these books. Each book contains 400 fun and challenging riddles that can provide very good mental stimulation for you and your kids and help make your minds develop even more.

Manufactured by Amazon.ca
Bolton, ON

10378667R00074